A book by

People Who Help People

by Jane Belk Moncure

illustrated by Helen Endres

Distributed by Childrens Press, 1224 West Van Buren Street, Chicago, Illinois 60607

Library of Congress Cataloging in Publication Data

Moncure, Jane Belk.
  People Who Help People

  SUMMARY: Introduces familiar community helpers such as teacher, ambulance driver, and dentist.

  1. Vocational guidance—Juvenile literature.
2. Service industries workers—Juvenile literature.
1. Vocational guidance I. Endres, Helen.
II. Title.
HF5381.2.M6   331.7'02   75-29225
ISBN 0-913778-16-8

People
Who Help
People

I am learning how to play
baseball.
My coach helps me.

I hit the ball by myself.
One day I will hit a homerun.
I know I will.

A coach may help you learn to swim.

A coach may help you learn how to play a new game.

People help people learn
all kinds of things.
My teacher is a helper.

She helps me and sometimes
I help her.

My father is a helper.
He helps me learn many
things such as how to build
a fire in the woods.

Firemen are helpers.
They help put out fires.
They help people escape
from burning buildings.

Policemen are helpers. They help
people who are in trouble.
If ever you are lost and
cannot find your way home,
ask a policeman to help you.
He will take you home again and
you will be safe.

Ambulance drivers are helpers.
They help people
who are sick or hurt.
If ever you are in an accident and
need to go to the hospital,
an ambulance driver will
take you there very quickly.

A doctor is a helper. A doctor helps people who are sick or hurt.

If you do not feel well,
go to see a doctor.
A doctor will help you
feel much better.

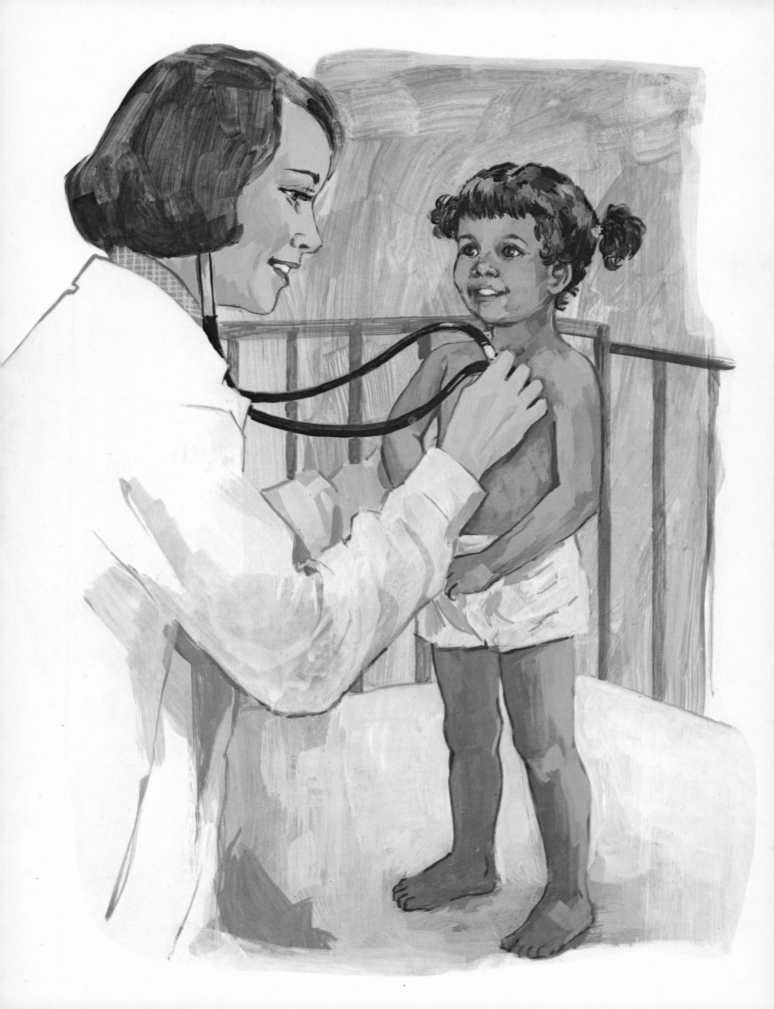

A dentist is a helper.
A dentist takes care of your teeth.
If you have a toothache, go
to see a dentist. He will help
you.

Even if you do not have a toothache,
visit the dentist and he will help
keep your teeth healthy.

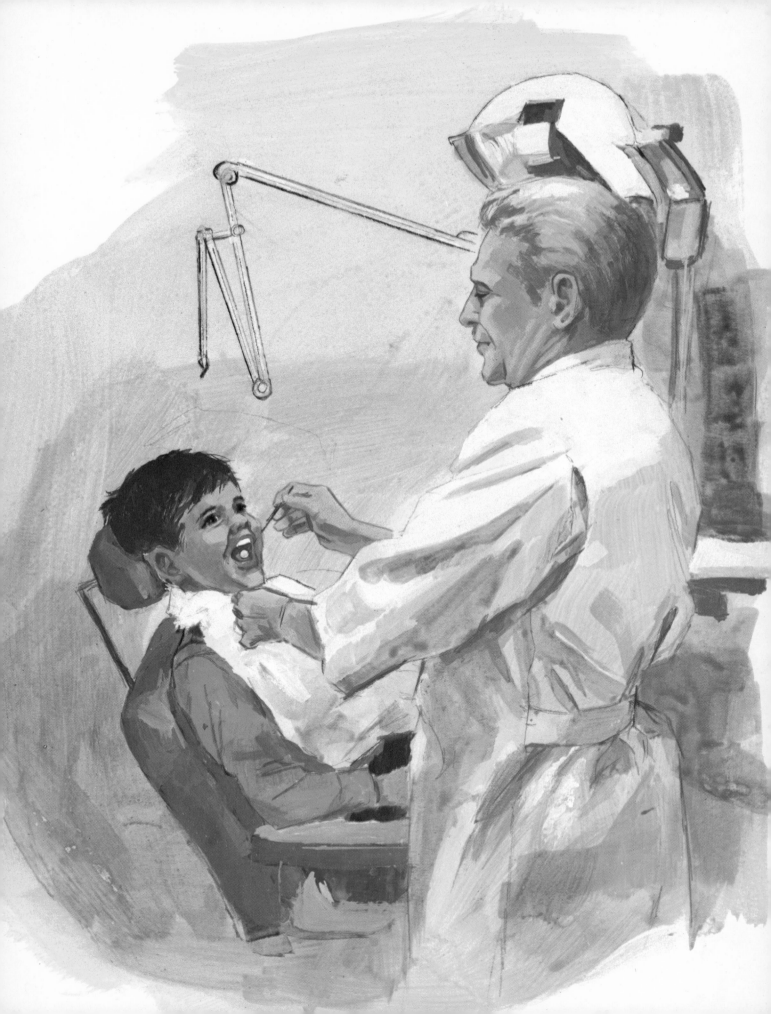

My brother is a helper.
He helps us cross the street in
front of our school. He stops
the traffic when the light is red.

I am a helper, too.
I help my mother buy groceries.
What kind of helper are you?

About the Author:

Jane Belk Moncure, author of many books and stories for young children, is a graduate of Virginia Commonwealth University and Columbia University. She has taught nursery, kindergarten and primary children in Europe and America. Mrs. Moncure has taught early childhood education while serving on the faculties of Virginia Commonwealth University and the University of Richmond. She was the first president of the Virginia Association for Early Childhood Education and has been recognized widely for her services to young children. She is married to Dr. James A. Moncure, Vice President of Elon College, and currently teaches in Burlington, North Carolina.